Festivals *of the* *World*

ENGLAND

Gareth Stevens Publishing
MILWAUKEE

Written by
HARLINAH WHYTE

Designed by
HASNAH MOHD ESA

Picture research by
SUSAN JANE MANUEL

First published in North America in 1997 by
Gareth Stevens Publishing
1555 North RiverCenter Drive, Suite 201
Milwaukee, Wisconsin 53212 USA

For a free color catalog describing Gareth
Stevens' list of high-quality books and multimedia
programs, call
1-800-542-2595 (USA)
or 1-800-461-9120 (Canada).
Gareth Stevens Publishing's Fax: (414) 225-0377.
See our catalog, too, on the World Wide Web:
http://gsinc.com

© TIMES EDITIONS PTE LTD 1997
Originated and designed by
Times Books International
an imprint of Times Editions Pte Ltd
Times Centre, 1 New Industrial Road
Singapore 536196
Printed in Singapore

Library of Congress Cataloging-in-Publication Data:
Whyte, Harlinah.
England / by Harlinah Whyte.
p. cm.—(Festivals of the world)
Includes bibliographical references and index.
Summary: Describes how the culture of England
is reflected in its many festivals, including the
Notting Hill Carnival, Lord Mayor's Day, and Guy
Fawkes Day.
ISBN 0-8368-1932-2 (lib. bdg.)
1. Festivals—England—Juvenile literature.
2 England—Social life and customs—Juvenile
literature. [1. Festivals—England. 2. England—
Social life and customs.] I. Title. II. Series.
GT4843.A2W49 1997
394.26941—dc21   97-9113

1 2 3 4 5 6 7 8 9 01 00 99 98 97

CONTENTS

It's Festival Time . . .

Did you know that Easter was named after an ancient goddess, or that the English celebrate a holiday to remember someone who tried to blow up their government building? England has ancient festivals that go back thousands of years, and newer festivals that came to the country from around the world. Come and dance around the Maypole, put on a Carnival mask, and meet the Queen. It's festival time in England . . .

WHERE'S ENGLAND?

E ngland is part of the island of Great Britain in western Europe. The country is famous for its green countryside, but most English people live in big cities. The capital is London.

England was once the center of the British Empire, which included large areas of North America, Africa, Asia, and Australia. Most of these areas are now independent nations.

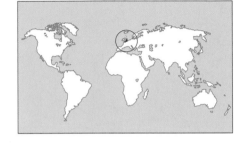

These schoolgirls are examples of the many different people you can see in England.

Who are the English?

The original inhabitants of the island were the **Celts** [kelts]. Long ago, the Celts were driven out of England by invaders from continental Europe. Over the centuries, the few Celts who remained mixed with the invaders to form the modern English. In more recent years, people have come to England from former British colonies, such as India, Pakistan, and parts of the Caribbean.

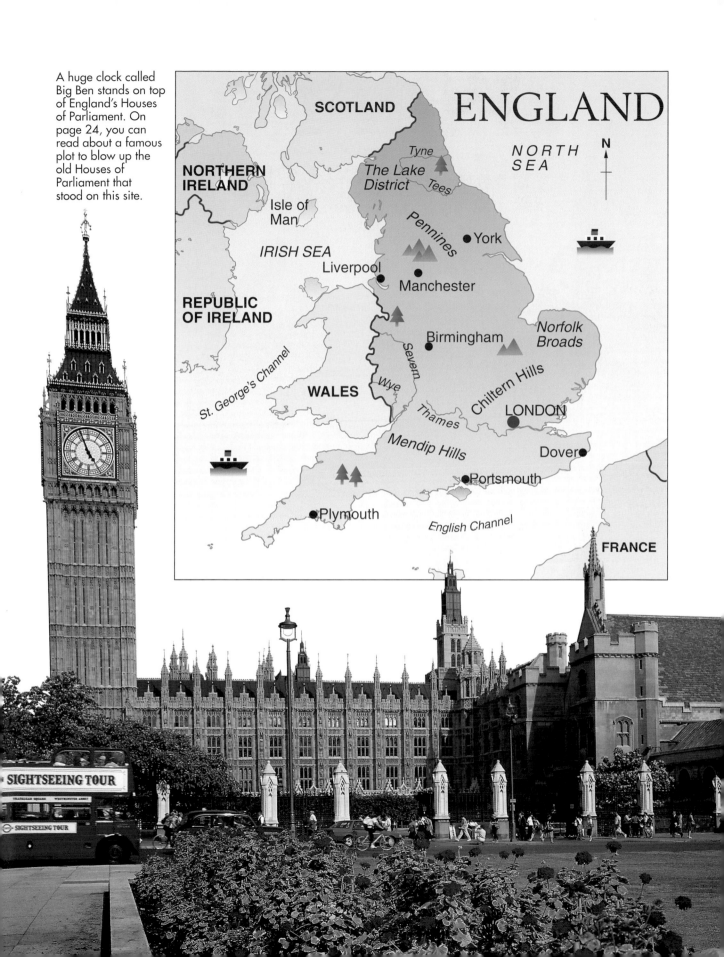

A huge clock called Big Ben stands on top of England's Houses of Parliament. On page 24, you can read about a famous plot to blow up the old Houses of Parliament that stood on this site.

ENGLAND

SCOTLAND

NORTH SEA

NORTHERN IRELAND

Isle of Man

IRISH SEA

REPUBLIC OF IRELAND

Tyne

The Lake District

Tees

Pennines

York

Liverpool

Manchester

Birmingham

Norfolk Broads

Severn

Wye

St. George's Channel

WALES

Chiltern Hills

Thames

LONDON

Mendip Hills

Dover

Portsmouth

Plymouth

English Channel

FRANCE

SIGHTSEEING TOUR

SIGHTSEEING TOUR

WHEN'S THE HOLIDAY?

Looking for some pomp and ceremony? Join us on page 16!

SPRING
- ✪ **PANCAKE DAY**
- ✪ **EASTER** ✪ **MAY DAY**
- ✪ **BELTANE**

SUMMER
- ✪ **NOTTING HILL CARNIVAL**
- ✪ **VILLAGE FAIRS**—Villages hold fairs, agricultural shows, and contests for charity.
- ✪ **HARVEST FESTIVALS**—Churches are decorated with agricultural crops to give thanks for the summer harvest.
- ✪ **QUEEN'S OFFICIAL BIRTHDAY**
- ✪ **DRESSING THE WELLS**—Large pictures made of flowers are placed next to wells to give thanks for the water supply.

Put on your costume and dance down to page 20 for the Notting Hill Carnival!

I'm Friar Tuck! Come and meet my friend Robin Hood at the May Day games on page 12.

AUTUMN

- ✪ **GUY FAWKES DAY**
- ✪ **LONDON TO BRIGHTON VINTAGE CAR RALLY**— A car race for cars built before 1905. It celebrates the raising of the speed limit from 4 to 12 miles (6 to19 km) per hour in 1896.
- ✪ **LORD MAYOR'S SHOW**
- ✪ **HALLOWEEN**
- ✪ **ARMISTICE DAY**—People wear red poppies and observe two minutes' silence to remember the soldiers who died in the World Wars. The Queen leads a procession of ex-soldiers.
- ✪ **PEARLY KINGS AND QUEENS**—In London, people dress in old-fashioned black clothes covered with patterns of pearly white buttons.

WINTER

- ✪ **HANUKKAH** ✪ **CHRISTMAS**
- ✪ **NEW YEAR'S DAY**
- ✪ **CHELSEA PENSIONERS' PARADE**
- ✪ **CHINESE NEW YEAR**—People gather in the streets to watch lion and dragon dances and set off fireworks.

EASTER

E aster is one of the most important festivals in the Christian calendar. It is the day when Christians celebrate the resurrection of Jesus Christ. But did you know that Easter comes from an ancient festival of spring? Keep reading and you'll find out how.

From Eostre to Easter

One of the groups of invaders that came to England many years ago was the **Anglo-Saxons.** They brought many of their customs with them. One of their customs was to celebrate the coming of spring at the end of the long, cold winter. Their goddess of spring was called **Eostre** [EAST-er]. Years later, the Anglo-Saxons became Christians. They worshiped Jesus Christ, but they never stopped practicing their old traditions in spring. Many of the Easter traditions celebrated in England today, such as giving eggs and Easter bunnies, come from the Anglo-Saxon festival. In fact, even the name of the holiday was handed down by the Anglo-Saxons!

Children look forward to receiving chocolate eggs and other Easter goodies.

Eggs and rabbits

Have you ever wondered why we eat eggs at Easter? Or why we talk about the Easter bunny? In the Anglo-Saxon tradition, the coming of spring was a time to celebrate new life. Eggs and rabbits are Anglo-Saxon symbols of life, birth, and fertility. Even though most people have forgotten the meaning behind eggs and rabbits, they still enjoy eating the chocolates delivered by the Easter bunny!

Hot cross buns

Have you ever eaten hot cross buns at Easter? They were also brought to us by the Anglo-Saxons. During the spring festival, an ox was sacrificed to the gods for a good harvest. Afterward, people celebrated by eating cakes with the mark of ox horns on top. The English word "bun" comes from the Anglo-Saxon word for ox. Later, the mark of the ox horns was thought to represent the sign of the cross on which Jesus Christ died.

The first one to roll an Easter egg to the end of the path will win this egg-rolling race!

Celebrating Easter

The day before Good Friday, the Queen hands out special coins to the poor. There is an extra coin each year because the number of coins is based on her age.

Good Friday is the day for breakfasting on delicious hot cross buns. Most Christians go to church on Good Friday, and some pray for three whole hours. This commemorates the time Christ hung on the cross. Easter Sunday is a day for fun. There are Easter egg hunts, egg-rolling contests, and lots of chocolate. If you're lucky, you may even see the Easter bunny!

Searching for eggs in the garden is one of the most exciting parts of Easter.

Queen Elizabeth II has been the Queen of England since 1952. In this picture she is attending a special Easter church service.

Pancake Day

In the past, Christians fasted during the day for the 40 days leading up to Easter. This period is called Lent. Some people still try to avoid eating rich foods, such as butter and eggs, during Lent. So, the day before Lent begins, Shrove Tuesday, they use up all the eggs and butter making pancakes! This is a popular celebration called Pancake Day. On this day, families get together to eat pancakes. The English like to eat pancakes with lemon juice and sugar instead of syrup. In English villages, people compete in pancake races, running while tossing pancakes in a frying pan. Although it is a long time before Easter, many people in England think of Pancake Day as the beginning of the Easter celebrations.

Getting ready for the pancake race. The competitors must be careful not to drop the pancakes as they run!

Think about this

According to an English legend, Pancake Day started more than 500 years ago. While a woman was making pancakes, she heard the church bells ringing. She dashed out of the house with her frying pan in hand and ran all the way to the church.

11

MAY DAY

May 1st is a public holiday in many countries. In some of those countries, it is known as Labor Day, a workers' holiday. In England, May 1st is called May Day, and it is a time to celebrate the beginning of summer.

Reviving the past

Girls dressed up for the May Day celebration.

The Celtic people of ancient England split the year into just two seasons—winter and summer. The first day of May marked the start of summer. On this day, a great festival was held to honor the returning sun. This festival was called Beltane, meaning "fire of God."

As Christianity spread across Europe, the May festival became a time for farmers to celebrate the coming season. Summer was the time when crops would grow and animals would have plenty to eat. Today, people in England celebrate May Day with many of the traditional dances and ceremonies of Beltane.

Opposite: It's easy to spot a morris dancer—you can't miss those hats!

Morris dancing is lively and colorful, and it always attracts a crowd of curious onlookers.

Let's dance!

Everyone knows it's May Day when they see **morris dancers**! You can tell who they are by their bright clothing, the flowers on their hats, and the bells on their legs. They wave ribbons, colored sticks, and bright scarves. The dances were traditionally performed by men to frighten away the evil spirits of winter. Today, women also join in the fun of the morris dance. Sometimes the dancers wear animal masks, and there is often a person dressed as a "hobby horse." The hobby horse attracts a huge crowd to watch its silly tricks. People walk through the streets all day long to watch the dancing and enjoy the party.

13

Round and round the Maypole

In villages and towns, dancing around the Maypole is a favorite part of May Day. The dance is taken directly from Beltane. After cutting down a tree and stripping off the branches, long, brightly colored ribbons were tied to the top of the trunk. Each dancer held a ribbon and skipped around the pole, moving in and out so that the ribbon wove a colorful pattern. Today, Maypole dancing is especially popular with children.

Robin Hood's Day

You've probably heard of the English folk hero, Robin Hood. Hundreds of years ago, his story became part of the May Day celebrations. As the village festival became fashionable in English cities, it expanded to include singers, bonfires, plays, archery competitions, and the choosing of a May King and May Queen. The May King dressed as Robin Hood, and the May Queen dressed as Maid Marian. Other people dressed as Robin Hood's merry men. In some places, May Day is still known as Robin Hood's Day.

Think about this
Some of the old Celtic festivals are still celebrated by people in England. These people are called Druids after the Celtic priests and teachers.

ROYAL PAGEANTRY

One of the special things about England is its royal family. Most English people enjoy the traditions that go with having a king or queen. The royal family's appointments are listed in the newspaper every day, and there are various public occasions when people can see members of the royal family. There are also traditional events with officials, such as the Lord Mayor of London. Even though Queen Elizabeth II does not have the same power as kings and queens who lived centuries ago, royal **pageantry** has kept its splendor, formality, and richness. Come and enjoy the show!

Even the drums and the horses wear rich and gorgeous costumes for royal events.

Trooping the Color

The Queen's birthday is in April, but since it sometimes clashes with Easter, her birthday is officially celebrated in June. On a Saturday in June, the Queen and other members of the royal family ride on horseback or in royal coaches to Horse Guards, an old stone building with a large parade ground. There the Queen inspects her personal guard. The display of troops is called Trooping the Color. Each **regiment** carries its own **color**, or special flag. The beautiful uniforms, soldiers on horseback, and rows of marching troops make this a very grand occasion. Thousands of people line the streets to watch the Queen's procession go by. There is not enough room for everyone to see the display at Horse Guards, so tickets are given away by lottery.

Above: It takes a lot of practice to get all these soldiers marching in perfect time.

A Horse Guard on duty.

17

The Lord Mayor rides in a gold state coach built in 1756.

Lord Mayor's Day

One of the most spectacular ceremonies in all of England is Lord Mayor's Day. Each year, a new Lord Mayor is elected to represent the city of London. In fact, this tradition has been going on for more than 900 years. On the second Saturday of November, the Lord Mayor dresses in special clothes and parades through London in a state coach. The coach is drawn by six horses. The 12 great city **livery companies** follow the coach in decorated floats.

In 1977, Queen Elizabeth II celebrated her Silver Jubilee—25 years as queen. All over England, people showed their patriotism by decorating their shops and homes with the **Union Jack** (the flag of the United Kingdom). In this village parade, the women are carrying symbols of each part of the United Kingdom: a rose for England, a thistle for Scotland, a daffodil for Wales, and a shamrock for Northern Ireland.

18

Chelsea Pensioners

Every February 16 there is a parade at the Royal Hospital Chelsea. This is a special hospital that looks after veterans (soldiers who have fought in wars). The hospital was founded by King Charles II, so today it is over 300 years old. Many of the veterans, who are known as Chelsea Pensioners, are over 80 years old. On their parade day, they wear their uniforms and all the medals they have won. As a special honor, they are greeted by a member of the royal family.

A Chelsea Pensioner stands proud in his military uniform.

Think about this

For the people of London, Lord Mayor's Day was once one of the most important days of the year. The day the new Lord Mayor took office, Londoners held a parade to show their loyalty to the king or queen.

NOTTING HILL CARNIVAL

S ince the 1950s, people from the Caribbean islands have been coming to live in England. Over the years, the Caribbean English have made very important cultural contributions. One of the most exciting is the Notting Hill Carnival, which takes place in London every year.

Parading through the streets for Carnival.

Carnival time!

The tradition of Carnival started centuries ago as a huge celebration in January or February. In the Caribbean (the islands between North and South America), the weather is warm at this time of year, so Carnival is celebrated outdoors. When immigrants came to England from the Caribbean, they missed their summer fun. So in August 1961, the people of Notting Hill in London held the first summer Carnival. It was a great success, and the crowds have been flocking to the Notting Hill Carnival ever since.

Left and right: Look at these amazing costumes! You can see hundreds of costumes like these at the Notting Hill Carnival.

The big party

The Notting Hill Carnival is a wonderful party! Men, women, and children dress up in elaborate costumes that sometimes take weeks to make. They dance through the streets in groups or ride on decorated floats. The groups of costumed dancers are called **mas** [MUSS] **bands**. *Mas* is short for masquerade. People from across England come to watch the mas bands. Sidewalk stalls serve all kinds of Caribbean specialities, such as goat curry.

This musician is beating a steel drum made from an old oil barrel.

Steel bands and calypso

Think about this

Do you like to dress up in fancy costumes and masks? Can you think of any other holidays when people dress up and wear masks?

Left: Sound systems are set up near the street, and people dance to all types of music.

Below: Mas bands compete to see who can come up with the most spectacular costumes, the best dance moves, and the cleverest theme.

At Carnival time, the streets are filled with the sound of drums, steel bands, and **calypso** [ca-LIP-so]. Calypso is a popular kind of music from the Caribbean.

The lively calypso melodies are played by steel bands. Steel drums were originally made from old oil barrels. A hammer was used to beat the end of the barrel into a curved drum head. Different notes are produced by striking different parts of the drum head. Even today, each steel drum is made by hand. Calypso and steel band music are part of Carnival's celebration of Caribbean culture. They are also great to dance to!

GUY FAWKES DAY

O n the fifth of November, the English celebrate a holiday unique to their country. Huge bonfires are built, dummies are burned on the fires, and fireworks are set off all over England. This festival had a very unusual start.

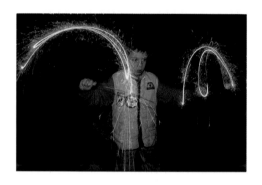

Making a pattern of light by waving sparklers.

Can you see the "guy" on top of this huge bonfire?

The Gunpowder Plot

In 1605, a group of Catholics led by Guy Fawkes tried to blow up the Houses of Parliament and kill King James. They were angry at the way the king treated Catholics. They hoped that by killing the king they could take control of the country. Fawkes and his men rolled 36 barrels of gunpowder under the Houses of Parliament. At the last moment the king was warned of the plot. Guy Fawkes and his group were captured and killed. Today, people remember this day with a rhyme:

Remember, remember, the fifth of November,
Gunpowder, treason, and plot.
We see no reason
Why gunpowder treason
Should ever be forgot!

24

Burning the Guy

Bonfires have been an important part of English festivals since the time of the Celts. Guy Fawkes Day is sometimes known as Bonfire Night. On Bonfire Night, people from neighborhoods, villages, and towns get together to watch the burning of Guy Fawkes. It's not really Guy Fawkes on top of the bonfire—it's a dummy made of old clothes stuffed with straw, newspaper, or rags. The dummy is simply called the **guy**.

In the evening, some children walk in the streets carrying the dummy and begging for "a penny for the guy." The children often use the money to buy firecrackers for the night. A fireworks display completes the evening.

These children are asking for "a penny for the guy."

25

THINGS FOR YOU TO DO

Do you celebrate the end of winter? After months of cold weather, it's good to see flowers, green grass, and blue skies. On May Day, English children like to celebrate with dancing and flowers. Here are some things you can do to make spring special.

Dance around a Maypole

An English May Day celebration is not complete without a Maypole. Making one is easy. Attach some crepe paper streamers or ribbons to a pole stuck in the ground or to a slender tree. You and your friends can each hold a ribbon and dance around singing:

Now we go round the maypole high,
Maypole high, maypole high.
Now we go round the maypole high,
Let the colored ribbons fly!

Make a May basket

Spring is the time for flowers. In some parts of England, children secretly deliver flowers to their friends and neighbors on May Day. They leave a small basket of flowers on the front step or hang them from the doorknob. You can make your own May basket. Shape a semicircle of paper into a cone, and glue or tape the seam. Punch holes in the sides and tie a piece of ribbon through the holes. Decorate the cone with paints, pens, or colorful pieces of paper. Before putting fresh flowers into the cone, wrap the stems with damp paper toweling and enclose the ends in a small plastic bag. This will keep the flowers fresh and stop the cone from getting wet. Now you can give your May basket to someone special!

Things to look for in your library

A Christmas Carol. Charles Dickens (Candlewick Press, 1993).
A Taste of Britain (Food Around the World). Roz Denny (Thomson Learning, 1994).
Dropping In on England. Lewis K. Parker (Rourke Publishing Group, 1994).
Easter Crafts: A Holiday Craft Book. Judith Hoffman Corwin (Franklin Watts, 1994).
England: A Country For All Time. (International Video Network).
Great Britain. (Journal Films and Video).
Kings and Queens. Phillipa Wingate (EDC Publications, 1995).
Queen of the May. Patience Brewster and Steven Kroll (Holiday House, 1993).
Robin Hood. (Baker and Taylor Video, 1991).

MAKE A GUY

On Guy Fawkes Day, every bonfire needs a guy. These stuffed figures represent Guy Fawkes, one of the conspirators who tried to blow up the Houses of Parliament. One guy can look very different from another—there is no fixed way to make them. You can make a guy using any kind of old clothes, and you can give it any face you like.

You will need:
1. A long-sleeved shirt
2. A pair of long pants
3. A pillowcase
4. Newspaper
5. A cap
6. A marker
7. String
8. A stapler

1 Stuff the shirt, pants, and pillowcase with scrunched-up newspaper. Tie off the pillowcase and the arms and legs with string.

2 Use the marker to draw a face on the pillowcase.

3 To assemble the guy, lay out the head, body, and legs, and tuck in the pillowcase and shirt. Staple the bottom of the pillowcase to the top of the shirt. Then staple the shirt to the pants. Give your guy a cap, and he's ready to go!

MAKE SCONES

E nglish people enjoy scones as an afternoon snack, often with a cup of tea. Scones are delicious with jam and whipped cream, or just with butter. They're best when they're freshly baked and still warm. This recipe makes about 12 scones.

You will need:

1. 2½ cups (280 g) self-rising flour
2. ⅓ cup (65 g) butter, cut into small pieces
3. ⅓ cup (65 g) sugar
4. 4 tablespoons milk
5. Pinch of salt
6. Extra flour
7. A mixing bowl
8. A sifter
9. A wooden spoon
10. Measuring cups
11. A board
12. A rolling pin
13. A round cutter
14. A baking tray
15. A wire rack
16. Potholders
17. Measuring spoons

1 Sift the flour and salt into a mixing bowl to get rid of any lumps. Rub the butter into the flour with your fingertips until the mixture is like breadcrumbs.

2 Add the sugar and milk and gently squeeze the mixture into a ball with your fingers.

3 Roll the mixture out onto a floured board until it is about 3/4 of an inch (2 cm) thick.

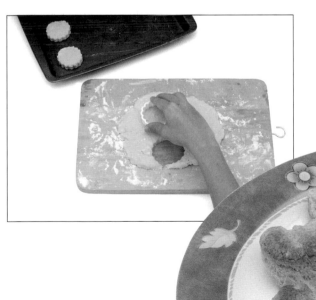

4 Cut circles out of the mixture with a round cutter. Put them onto a greased baking tray. Bake your scones at 425°F (220°C) for about 10 minutes, until brown on top. Leave them to cool on a rack.

GLOSSARY

Anglo-Saxons, 8   The Angles and Saxons, tribes from Denmark and Germany who settled in England nearly 1,500 years ago.

calypso, 23   A popular Caribbean musical form.

Celts, 4   The original inhabitants of Great Britain.

color, 17   A special flag that marks each regiment of soldiers.

Eostre, 8   The Anglo-Saxon goddess of spring.

guy, 25   A dummy made of old clothes that is burned on a bonfire.

livery companies, 18   Traditional trade and craft associations in London. The workers wear livery (special clothing) on formal occasions.

mas bands, 22   Groups of dancers who parade through the streets during Carnival.

morris dancers, 13   Traditional dancers at the May Day celebrations.

pageantry, 16   Grand, formal displays and ceremonies.

regiment, 17   An organized unit of soldiers.

Union Jack, 18   The flag of the United Kingdom.

INDEX

Picture Credits
Camera Press: 2, 10 (bottom), 13 (bottom), 16; Haga Library, Japan: 11; Hutchison Library: 4, 7 (top), 12, 24 (top); International Photobank: 5, 6, 7 (bottom), 17 (bottom); Life File: 1, 10 (top), 19, 20 (both), 21, 22 (top); Photobank: 17 (top), 23; David Simson: 3 (top), 8, 18 (bottom), 24 (bottom), 25; Topham Picture Point: 18 (top), 22 (bottom), 26, 28; Travel Ink: 3 (bottom), 9 (top), 13 (top), 14, 15; Trip: 9 (bottom)